Atwood Hall: The Federal Prison Camp for Women in Lexington, Kentucky

So you have been sentenced to a Federal Prison Camp (FPC). It seems like the end of the world but it isn't. Most camps are more akin to a college dorm situation than a real prison. One thing I can tell you with 100% certainty is that it is nothing like you have seen on television so stop watching those shows and scaring the crap out of yourself.

For starters, if any television show based itself on life at a prison camp it probably wouldn't last 3 episodes; camps are pretty boring. Second of all, the Feds definitely don't want people seeing the waste of their tax dollars that are camps. So unless you know someone who has been to one or you have visited the website PrisonTalk.com, you really have no idea what to expect. That's why I wrote this.

When I was sentenced to a little over a year in the FPC in Lexington, Kentucky, I had no idea what to expect. I'm not a lifetime criminal by any stretch of the imagination. In fact my paperwork says that I have "no criminal versatility" and my security score was so low that it had to be bumped up enough to get me into the camp. Unfortunately there was little to no information on this particular camp on the Internet and my attorney was also clueless.

As a writer, I decided to write a guide to the Lexington camp specifically and prison camps in general. While the information is specific to Lexington, it will apply to other camps as well. Variation would require creativity, thought and ambition. Those three elements are missing in the Federal system; especially thought.

While I was in Lexington, it became common knowledge that I would eventually write a book about the experience. After more than a year at home I have hopefully put enough distance between the events and myself to be fair and charitable. Just don't count on it.

This is important, so please pay attention:
I know you are scared. Unlike many who write guides, I have been exactly where you are right now. I can tell you this, with no fear of being wrong: You will be safe at Lexington. The same is true of the other camps as well. No violence of any kind is tolerated for a second. Violent offenders are not sent to camps. Aggressive offenders are not sent to camps. The people at the camps are just like you. They made a mistake but they aren't bad people. **YOU ARE GOING TO BE OK**. I promise. Right now is as bad as it gets. It all gets better from here.

Believe it or not, I made some really great friends in Lexington. People I actually miss. To give you an idea of how bad the camps can be: I even miss some of the staff. That's right, I miss them. They are really great people and despite what you have seen on television they are not out to get you. They aren't your friends while you are in there; they have a job to do. But they make things as easy for you as you let them.

So on with the guide!

Self-Surrender

This has got to be the most bullshit idea ever conceived by the government. The very idea that they tell me to take myself to prison AND I GO is so far-fetched that it would never fly in a novel. Yet on any given day hundreds of people actually voluntarily arrive at prisons across the country.

The big question is what can you take when you self-surrender? The truth is that the answer varies from camp to camp and month to month. I was told, by Lexington, to take nothing. Any money would have to be sent via Western Union. When I arrived, the perimeter officer told us I could take money. So I walked in with the money instead of having it sent. You can wear in a wedding band (solid with no gems) and a cross or other religious necklace (no gems).

The entire idea of self-surrender gets even weirder when you consider that there are thousands of inmates transferring from one prison to another all alone thanks to Greyhound Bus Lines. That's right. People with a longer prison term or those in a medium security prison being sent to a camp will get on the bus by themselves and go to the next prison.

Receiving and Discharge (R&D)

At Lexington, R&D is located at the actual medical facility known to the camp as "A" building. A little explanation is needed here. Don't panic and freak out when you see the razor wire, big old fence and armed officers. All Federal Medical Prison facilities are high security. That doesn't mean that those who are there are all problems, but the medical facility has to take ill prisoners from all over so they have to be at the standard of the highest level offender that is likely to be there for treatment. In Lexington this is a male facility. You will not be staying there except for R&D, which lasts a couple of hours. You will not see the male inmates.

You walk through the doors and tell them who you are. They will take a photo of you for your prison ID card and re-fingerprint you. This is primarily to make sure that you are who you say you are. You will give them your money and they will give you a receipt. The money will be credited to your commissary account within 2 days. You will then sit in an unlocked holding room while you fill out paperwork. You will also be given your prison handbook.

I read my handbook because I had nothing better to do. It was less than worthless. I kept it because at this point the only personal possessions I had were a pen and that handbook.

Then you get a cursory medical exam. They checked my blood pressure and asked several routine medical questions. Then I went back to the holding area. A little later I was taken by a nice female officer to get my official "welcome to prison" outfit. This consisted of khaki pants, a white sports bra, white underwear and a white t-shirt. I was also given a pair of slip-on blue moccasins. I had to completely undress, squat and cough, and redress with the female officer present. She paid about as much attention to me as I did to her. I met her several other times throughout my stay there and can tell you that she is one of the single nicest people I have ever met anywhere and is one of those perpetually happy people. So is her husband who also works there. I was given my bedroll and sent back to the holding area until a town driver came to get me.

Town drivers are one of my favorite parts of camp life. The town driver is an inmate that has a driver's license and keys to a government vehicle. They drive people all over the camp and, most importantly, to the train-bus-airport when the times comes to leave. After they drive you to the bus they go back to the camp. I suppose once you self-surrender returning to the camp is pretty much a given. It's still kind of strange.

Arrival at Camp

After you walk through the front doors you will be taken to the officer's station for sign in and to be given your "don't make me do any paperwork" lecture. Because the officers rotate between buildings, I can't promise you will get Tussey that first day. I was lucky that I did. He's a great guy and a good person to vent to if you feel the need. Just don't make him do any paperwork or lie to his face and you will get along just fine. Whatever officer is there when you arrive, it will be someone nice. I knew them all and they were all really great people, not a jerk in the bunch. One of my favorites was an afternoon officer named Crook. I thought the name was perfect for an officer in a Federal prison.

You will be told what time to come down after dinner to get clothing to last you until dress-out on Friday. You will also get a pillow. The afternoon officer is the one to see about this. Just wander up to the door, tell him you are new and supposed to get stuff from laundry. They will take care of the rest.

Welcome to Prison – My First Afternoon

The town driver came and took me over to the building where I would spend the next 14 months. It's also known as Atwood Hall, which has kind of a prep school ring to it, in a rather warped way. From the front it's really very pretty. There are tons of beautiful flowers and it's very friendly looking. You walk through the front doors and go into the office on your left. If you are paying attention you will notice that is says "Officer's Station" on the wall over the door in rather funky script. This is where I met the bald guy that smelled good. His name is Tussey. He is what is referred to as a Kentucky good-ole boy. His job is to give you a brief lecture and then hand you over to the tour guide.

The lecture is pretty standard stuff. Stay out of trouble is the main theme. He told me to "stay away from that lesbian shit" and "Don't make me do any paperwork" several times. I later found out that this was his idea of a joke to new people. I eventually told him that he was scaring the crap out of people and to knock it off. He did tone it down quite a bit after that. He didn't fully grasp the emotional disconnect that new inmates have upon arrival. It's hard to get humor at that point. In fact, don't be surprised if you have problems understanding the people who are laughing and smiling. It's hard to imagine that you will ever smile again but you will.

Tussey suggested that I buy a radio both to listen to music and to watch television. To hear the television you have to tune your radio to certain stations. Listening to music is a popular way to pass the time. For me it was to help drown out noise.

There is A LOT of noise in this place. According to friends in there, it was pretty much a normal level for prisons. Even so, more than a year later, I'm still working on getting my hearing back. One of the best gifts I was given when I arrived in Lexington was a pair of earplugs. You can buy them in the commissary and I highly recommend them. I used to wear mine all day at times. It made for much nicer days.

The tour guide then gave me a guided tour of the building. Normally, the tour starts at your room. Contrary to popular belief, there are no cells in camps. There certainly are no cells at the Lexington camp. It's also a common belief that everyone starts in what is called "The Bus Stop." The truth is that you will be put where they have space. In my case, I was actually in what is called an open bus stop. Ok, it was formerly a day room but they ran out of space and put beds in there. When it was full, there were 25 of us in there. It's a huge room and I never felt cramped. I put my bedroll on my bunk and continued with the tour.

The tour started officially with the 3rd floor. What was of interest to me, according to Allison my guide, was the beauty shop and one of the 3 laundry rooms. There was also a TV room up there. We moved on to the second floor where there was another laundry room, another TV room, the offices of the two counselors and the computers. The first floor had the final laundry room, chapel, religious library, phone room, rest of the staff offices and cafeteria. The basement held the movie room, library, game room, commissary, unit laundry (for getting new bedding, clothes etc.) and the main library.

Allison took me back to my bunk and asked one of the ladies in the room to show me to dinner. It was almost count time and she had to go to her own room.

When I returned to my bunk I found that my bed had been made. I'm tall but the young lady who made my bed for me made me feel short. At over 6 feet tall, Tasha was the tallest in the camp. She taught me how to make a camp bed (there are no fitted sheets) by tying knots in my sheets. The others had put snacks and other things like shampoo, soap and deodorant on my bed. This is the norm in camps. Everyone remembers what it was like when they first arrived and had nothing. You pay it back by doing the same thing later for other new arrivals. One woman, Cindy, had an extra plastic drinking mug that she gave to me. It was my only way to drink anything other than use the water fountain.

At 4pm, more or less, I heard someone yell "COUNT" and everyone stood up by their bunk. Two officers came through and counted us. After they finished with our floor they yelled "CLEAR" and we were free to move about the floor. Once the building was clear one of my new friends, Cindy, forced me to go to dinner. Cindy is a tiny little person and very motherly. She and a woman named Valarie insisted that I needed to eat something. I went with them to the first floor and got into line.

At about 4:30 the cafeteria opened up and we went in to eat. I picked at the food. After dinner we went to our room. Mail Call was a 6pm and then again at 8pm. A little before 6pm a mail sheet was posted on the wall. You could check and see if your name was highlighted on it, letting you know you had mail. I didn't have any that first night so I went to take a shower and then went to bed. Yes, I cried myself to sleep that night. I cried myself to sleep for a month, maybe longer.

That's enough of that crap, back to the Guide!

The First Day – What you need to know about what you need to do

If you read the handbook you are actually behind the curve. The handbook is, as I said earlier, less than worthless. Here is how things really work:

Callout Sheets

Callout sheets are printed sheets that tell campers (which is actually how they refer to us) what their appointments are for the next day. Technically speaking you are supposed to be at whatever appointments are listed or you can get a shot. The reality is that if you aren't there the person will just send a runner to find you and tell you to get to wherever it is you are supposed to be. These sheets also detail any job changes you might have.

According to the handbook, the callout sheet is posted at 4pm. That never, even once, happened. The reality is that the sheet is usually dropped off by the last stand up count officer. Normally he puts it in the windowsill by the main doors to each floor. About half of the time I would actually go down and get it from him at the officer's station after count cleared. Sometimes it hadn't been brought over from "A" building and I hung out with others waiting for it. I didn't want to go to bed until I knew I didn't have to be up for anything specific the next day.

It's considered good form to check for your roommates as well as yourself when you are in a room smaller than the bus stop. When I was in the Penthouse I would get the callout sheet from the officer, scan for the names of my roommates and had the sheet over to someone else. Then I would announce the finding to the room when I returned. This was much easier when I was moved to the 5-star suite; there were only 3 of us in there.

Your First Morning

You get up around 7am. There was no alarm, general call or anything else. People start getting up and making noise. Until you get acclimated, the noise of the others will wake you. You can buy an alarm clock in the commissary but frankly the alarms are so soft on them it wouldn't have worked for me anyway.

When you get up, make your bed. You will learn some very odd things in prison and one of those is that once you make your bed, you don't unmake it except to do laundry. You sleep on top of the made bed using your extra blanket for a cover. Then in the morning you fold up the extra blanket and place it across the bottom of your bed. Or at least you did until they took our extra blankets. After that we stored them in our lockers or placed them over the other blanket on the made bed. Just do what your roommates are doing in regards to this.

On the off chance you care, Breakfast is served from 6:30 until 7:30 in the morning. Most of the time breakfast consists of cereal, donuts or energy bars. There is also coffee and milk. You can buy your own cereal in the commissary and they also have pop tarts. You heat the pop tarts in the microwave for 10-15 seconds.

Morning sign in was always a crapshoot while I was there and depends entirely on the officer and what he or she requires. Some make you sign in with your ID (ok, to be fair this happened twice). Most of the time there is just a sheet of paper on the mailbox and you sign it. On Fridays it was customary for the officer to wander around and check off our names that way. It's supposed to be signed by 8:30 am. I missed signing in more often than not. Doing so would have interfered with my morning nap.

Dressing Out and Clothing Matters

On your first Friday you will go down to the main laundry area of the camp. After standing in line for a bit you will be given the rest of your clothing and your "greens," the official prison uniform: forest green pull-on pants and shirt; with your name and number on them. You will also be given your steel-toed boots. Unless you want to wash dishes or work outside during your visit, try and get a soft shoe pass. Then you can get rid of the damned boots. I wore mine twice and then won the Atwood Lottery and never had to wear them again.

You are required to wear your greens from 7:30 until 3:30pm on the first floor. During late spring through summer, the unit manager allows those working in the building to wear only the white t-shirt instead of both the shirt and vest. On evenings and weekends you could wear your grays. Grays are the gray shorts or sweatpants that you buy in the commissary. Unless you have a soft-shoe pass (no one ever asked to see mine) you had to wear boots on the first floor during those hours as well. Orderlies were never required to wear the boots while working or the green vest, a point in favor of Ms. Sloan.

With the exception of the dining room, you also have the option to wear your sandals after working hours and on weekends. No one wears greens on weekends unless they want to do so or have a visit.

Medical Care

You are most likely going to be on the callout sheet that first day. You will go to medical for a more complete evaluation and a TB test. Within 2 weeks you will be on the callout sheet for blood work. You have the option to refuse this and I did. I hate needles and refusing was simply not a problem.

A lot has been said and written elsewhere about the horrible state of medical care you get in federal prison. I can't agree. Both the doctor and his PA were outstanding. I was treated extremely well and given very good care the few times I needed it. If I could, I would have Doctor Clancy as my regular physician. He's a very kind and gentle man who was almost as happy I was going home as I was. His office staff was no different.

Keep in mind that as someone who generally doesn't go see a doctor until I have absolutely no choice, I wasn't sitting in sick call every day to get out of work. They only saw me long after I should have gone to see them. If you are constantly parked on the bench outside their office or trying to get drugs then you are not going to have the same experience that I had.

I quickly won the Atwood Lottery because I have plantar fasciitis and asthma. This means that I was given a soft shoe pass along with an elevator pass and an extra pillow.

If you are given a medical exception form, such as I had for the winning of the Atwood lottery, you will need to keep a copy on your locker. You can get tape for this from the library.

By the time your medical appointments are complete, it should be about lunchtime. Lunch is from 11:30 to 12:30. Lunch is the only time of day you get dessert. Cookies are popular and so is the banana pudding. Since I left they have brought back the salad bar. Wednesday is hamburger day. It's ALWAYS hamburger day. Many people count their time based on how many hamburger days they have left.

During your tour you were given a psychological survey form. After you fill it out slip it under the door of the psychologist. She's a nice lady but rather clueless about what we go through. Humor her; it makes the time go faster.

The afternoon sign in sheet should be where the morning one was. I rarely signed that one either. It interfered with my early afternoon nap.

Your First Afternoon

You have now been in prison nearly 24 hours. You have the afternoon ahead of you with nothing to do. Go to the library. You don't normally hit the A&O sheet until the second day you are there (more on that later) so you might as well go to the library. You have two library choices. The religious library is on the first floor next to the psychologist's office. The libraries will close at 3:30 to give everyone time to get back to her room in time for 4pm count. Or you can take a nap. Someone will wake you for the stand up count.

Count Times and Significance

There are two stand-up counts Monday through Friday at 4pm and 9pm. You stand up by your bunk and the officers count you. The object of this is to make sure you are alive. The other count times are midnight, 3am and 5am. On weekends there is a 10am stand up count added into the mix.

DO NOT MISS COUNT

Missing count is a bad thing and the consequences depend entirely on the mood of the officers. It can be everything from extra duty, a shot, a trip to county or nothing at all. Most of the time an apology goes a long way. I missed count at 3am once because I got up and wandered into the bathroom not knowing what time it was. I came out of the bathroom to find them counting. They quietly asked me to stand where I was, completed the count of the room, added me into it and left. Nothing more was ever said.

You have now made it through your first day in prison. It gets far more boring from here on out. The best advice I was given was to get into a routine. That helps the time go faster. You will read a LOT in prison. Learn to crochet and/or knit. Those are very popular pastimes. Unless you have less than 6 months you will eventually break down and learn to crochet. Everyone always does.

Good Time Credit

One of the first questions you will have when you hear about your sentence is how much of it you will actually have to serve. There are several online calculators where you can compute this. Take care to select the federal option instead of your state. Each state tends to compute the number differently and if you are heading to prison on a federal charge then the only one that matters is theirs. At camps, getting your Good Time Credit (GTC) is pretty much a given. Unless you get into serious trouble you can count on having these days reduced from your overall sentence.

You will see two numbers bantered about a lot: 54 and 47. While the law states that prisoners get 54 days of GTC in reality, due to a glitch in the way the law was written, this actually amounts to 47 days per year. You can fuss and argue this all you want but it is what it is and until this is changed you will get 47 days of GTC per year.

Wait, it gets better. To get ANY days off of your sentence you have to serve more than one year in prison. This is why you so frequently see sentences of a year and a day. That extra day means everything. If you are sentenced to a flat year in prison then you will do every single day of that sentence. If you are given a year and a day then you will be home 47 days sooner.

Typically, within a week of arriving at Atwood Hall you will be sent a letter giving you the information regarding your release date. This date is the absolute last date that the Bureau of Prisons can hold you in either prison or a half-way house. After that you're either conditionally released on supervised release or simply released.

One tidbit you will hear a lot about while in Atwood Hall is that they are revising the Good Time Credit rules to give you more time off for good behavior. This is a popular prison myth that is not currently being discussed in Congress.

Speaking of time, I want to impart to you something called "Inmate Time" that was told to me by a friend, Kristy. We lived in the Bus Stop together and I loved her for her humor and her desire to walk enough miles on the walking track to have made it home. Between the walking and eating nothing but Tuna for a few months she lost about 40 pounds. She explained to me about Inmate Time to help me feel better one night when I had been obsessing over my calendar and how much time I had left.

Inmate Time is calculated by ignoring the current month....because it's going to go by fast. Then you ignore the month you leave because it will also go by fast. February is a really short month so it should be almost ignored. Right there you lose 3 months off your sentence! I know it has no basis in logic and is completely insane. However when it's presented to you by a friend trying to make you feel better and who is really excited about it, well it almost makes sense.

Working in Prison

Contrary to popular belief, there are forced labor camps in the United States. In America, we call them prisons. You are going to get a job in prison. Accept that fact and move on. The question is what kind of job.

There were several types of jobs in Lexington. I was a very short timer who from the very beginning was counting her time in months, not years. I attended my first pre-release class less than a month after arriving.

You are most likely going to be underemployed at Lexington. I can't speak for other camps, but when I was there the population never went above 300 and there simply wasn't enough work to go around. As of this writing the population is up to 356.

Everything you read and hear says that you will do 90 days in the kitchen. As I already mentioned, that isn't true. I never saw the kitchen. None of my friends did either. You can ask for a job change if you don't like the assignment. Jobs like the shop and landscaping pay better but that wasn't an issue for me so I stayed with the orderly position I was given and left it at that. I was able to work from 7:30 in the morning until 8:00 in the morning. It was one of the few things that didn't interfere with my napping.

You will get paid for the work you do but good luck in figuring out the pay scale. The best paying jobs are reserved for those with more time to serve and they might make $35 a month. I had money coming in from home every month and I made $25 on average from my job as an orderly because my boss liked me. I think the minimum you can get is $5.50 a month.

Admission and Orientation (A&O)

Normally the second day after you arrive you will be on the A&O list. No one told me about this so when I started doing the tours, I made sure to tell new arrivals about the list. When you are A&O you will be assigned to help clean the building. The joke was that A&O stands for Assist the Orderlies. Orderlies clean the place. A&O people are supposed to help the orderlies do the job, not do it for them. I always stressed this because so many inmates would try and get the new people to do their jobs for them. There is a sheet posted outside the office of the counselor in charge of the orderlies. Look for your name and ask someone who the other people on that line are and where that area of the building is located. Someone will be happy to show you. The day will come when you will be the person asked. Please remember how you felt and be nice to them. It helps a lot. You will go to that spot and help clean it up. Orderlies start work at 7:30 and finish at 3pm; officially. As A&O once you are done with the morning cleaning, you are done for the day. Actual orderlies have to go back every now and then to spot check. I was an orderly and I was back in bed and asleep before 8am every day when I didn't have a new person to help. When I did have extra help I was asleep by 7:45.

Depending on when you arrive, you and all of the other new people will be on the callout sheet for the A&O meeting. I happened to arrive the afternoon of one of those meetings so mine came two weeks later. This turned out to be a good thing.

On the day of the meeting you will go to the basement room that doubles as the visitation room. You will spend the morning listening to a parade of staff members telling you about the camp. After lunch you will go back and hear the rest of them. Then you will watch a video that, if you saw it the first day, would scare you. It's a sexual abuse video that shows a woman offering another woman a cookie and it's clear that this is a prelude to sexual favors. Nothing like this ever went on in Lexington and I doubt it goes on in the other camps. The bottom line is that while sexual activity certainly goes on, it's entirely consensual. There are more than enough willing partners. The meeting will be over by around 2pm. One thing, try to not roll your eyes every time you hear the staff tell you that it's a "privilege" for you to be in the camp. They don't care and it will give you a headache. Ditto for how "lucky" you are to be there.

Within a couple of days after the meeting you will be assigned a job at the camp. If you would prefer one job to another, go and see the boss in charge of them. The handbook and everyone else will tell you that you have to work in the kitchen for 90 days before getting another job. This isn't true. I never worked in the kitchen and none of my friends did either. I was immediately assigned as an orderly. It was all in all a great job. I worked for 15 minutes a day, made $25 a month and slept the rest of the time; my boss liked me. She rarely saw me, but she liked me.

Staff – Who they are and what they do

Officers

You will generally only see two daily in Lexington. The day officer is there from 7:30am until 3:30pm. The evening officer is there from 3:30pm until bedtime. The overnight officer is rarely seen, though you may see him or her early in the morning.

The official purpose of the officers is to count us and keep us under control. The reality, in Lexington camp, is that they are highly paid glorified babysitters who have little to do other than the required counting. If you are having a problem you can go to them. For the most part, what Tussey said was true. If you respect them and don't make them do any paperwork, you will get along fine. I actually liked all of the officers that were there. I never had a problem with any of them and I don't know anyone who did. They were polite, funny and treated us with respect.

Counselors

There were two when I arrived. Each is assigned roughly half of the inmates. They deal with your life inside Lexington. They are who you see if you have a problem, to get visitors approved and for pretty much anything else that concerns your life in prison. The two that were there when I was were Rebecca Brown and Sharon Sloan. Ms. Brown was my counselor. Ms. Sloan was my boss.

Case Managers

There are also two of them and they pair up with the counselors. If you have Ms. Brown for your counselor then you always have Ms. Miller for your case manager. The running joke was that they paired up the best case manager with the worst counselor and the best counselor with the worst case manager.

Case managers deal with your release. These are the people who set your halfway house time, deal with your release plans and so forth. They are the ones to see about matters that deal with life outside the prison.

Unit Manager

There were two while I was there, Ms. Ward and Mr. White. Mr. White had the annoying habit of telling everyone how lucky we were to be there. Other than that he was a great guy. Ms. Ward was a nice lady and very energetic. I only had a couple of dealings with her but she was cool. The unit manager makes sure the building runs smoothly.

Medical personnel

The doctor, PA, dentist and psychologist make up the medical staff. Their roles are pretty self-explanatory. The psychologist also tends to run the majority of the classes there. There are classes in parenting, drug abuse and so on.

Commissary Officer

This is the officer that runs the commissary. Both of them were nice guys. Don't give them a hard time and they won't give you one. They made it a point of knowing when we were leaving and wishing us well.

Education Officer

He runs the education office, such as it is. At Lexington there was nothing they could offer me. While getting your GED is required for those who didn't graduate high school, if you have a college degree then there is really nothing much that this facility can offer. I met him twice and by all accounts he's a nice guy.

The one really important thing you need to understand about the staff is that they are first and foremost Federal Employees. Their primary goal is to get through their jobs and collect their retirement with as little hassle as possible. They don't rock the boat and the only time they really care what you are doing is if it is going to create problems for them. Don't bother them and they will not bother you.

The Outstanding Officers of Atwood Hall

I spent 15 months in Atwood Hall. I met women from prisons all over the nation, both state and federal. The general consensus was that the officers will treat you with respect if you treat them with respect. I never heard of or saw a problem with the guards in Lexington.

In Lexington, every 3 months or so, the officers rotate between the buildings to prevent burnout. Part of it is because the men have everything from medium to maximum security inmates and that is stressful on the officers. The other part is that being a glorified babysitter for around 300 women is even more stressful than maximum security males. We don't fight or riot; we bitch and nag.

In those 15 months there were officers that were incredibly wonderful, funny and kind. They made a bad situation much more bearable and even enjoyable. My advice for dealing with them is to be honest, don't give them trouble, and don't make them do any paperwork. There were several standouts. Many are still there. Believe it or not, I miss them. They are great people.

The Infamous Sloan

One of the first things people warned me about in Lexington was one of the counselors, Sharon Sloan. They told me to avoid her like the plague. I actually got along with her when I saw her. Most of the time I tended to avoid her. I was usually busy napping.

About 7 weeks after I arrived, Lexington experienced a heat wave. It was 106 degrees outside and not any better inside. Lexington is not air-conditioned and inmates have to use small fans purchased from the commissary that do not work well. The institution itself provides several industrial fans that help some, but mostly just add to the noise and move hot air around. It was not unusual for inmates to get their shirts wet before attempting to sleep. There were signs posted all over the building "How to survive a heat wave." It was miserable.

On one of these days Ms. Sloan decided to punish the orderlies because she thought that we weren't cleaning enough. Her punishment was to send the entire crew out in the hot sun wearing full greens and order us to pick clover flowers while wearing latex gloves. Being in the direct sun, within a few minutes we started getting sick. We had no access to water and the heat index was above 110. It's important to note that 95% of the inmates are on antidepressants making it even more dangerous to get overheated. My asthma starts to both me and I decided to go inside to get my inhaler. I never made it.

I started to collapse just inside the door and was taken to medical by the officer as I began shivering and passed out. I'm well cared for and within an hour I make a good recovery. The medical team is furious when I tell them what made me (and now 15 others) so ill. The day officer was also furious.

The next morning Sloan does it again. This time I ignore the call to go out and wander off. It was a Wednesday morning.

Every Wednesday the senior staff, including the warden, would make themselves available to the inmates during lunch. If you have an issue that you need to discuss with them, you are welcome to do so. Either the officer or the medical staff (perhaps both) had complained to the warden about us being out in the sun for the bullshit purpose of picking clover flowers. The Warden arrived early. She arrived to see what was going on and ordered the inmates back into the building and back to their real jobs. She was furious.

The warden is not the type to mince words and half of the building heard her yelling at Sloan. She called Sloan a disgrace, inhumane and a pathetic excuse for a human being. She forbade anything like that from ever happening again. It never did.

In late October Sloan was irritated again and had us outside cleaning assorted things like the mop buckets. It was a great day and no one really minded. We had water fights and it was fun. At one point she asked me to go and find 2 missing buckets. I could only find one and sent it outside with the others while I searched for the escaped bucket. I found it along with the orderly who was in charge of cleaning that area:

Me: Hey! Sloan wants me to take the bucket out to be cleaned with the others.
Inmate: Yah cain't have mah bucket!

Me: I don't want your bucket, Sloan wants the bucket to be cleaned and so we can oil the wheels.
Inmate: She cain't have mah bucket neither! It's MAH bucket and da wheels works jest fine.
Me: Okay, I'll tell her.

I went out and explained the problem with Ms. Sloan who was making rainbows with the water from the hose. She sprayed me as I approached and I sprayed her back after wrenching the hose from her. We were laughing as we walked back into the building for lunch a few minutes later. Ms. Sloan said that she couldn't understand what gets into some people. I told her that she was probably just paranoid that her boss might go psycho and make her pick clover flowers in the heat. Ms. Sloan was laughing when she told me that she had punished her daughter along those lines when she was a kid. I told her she was very brave considering that her daughter is an only child and therefore going to be solely responsible for the nursing home choice. Ms. Sloan found that very funny and was in a great mood when we parted.

Yes, Ms. Sloan could be a bitch and annoy the hell out of people. But she was generally a nice person and would go out of her way to help you if she could. For some reason, perhaps because my friend Mary put in a good word for me, Sloan liked me. She tended to leave me alone most of the time and was very nice when I got sick, even coming to my room to check on me. She retired a few months after my release and I really hope she is enjoying her free time.

Tales of Tussey

I don't know anyone that doesn't love this guy! He was funny, obnoxious, and an all-around great guy. He came around and checked on me several times during the first few days. It wasn't until much later that I realized what he was doing. He was that kind of guy. Shortly before I left my roommate and I had an argument. She's a pain in the ass on a good day and decided to tell Tussey that something was wrong with me because I was napping so much and a little while later he came to my room where I was sleeping. The height of the bunk placed us at eye level when I was asleep. I opened my eyes to find him grinning at me. I laughed and told him I had been there so long that opening my eyes to find him looking at me no longer startled me. He laughed and told me to come see him when I had a chance. I went down a bit later and he told me what Popeck had said and asked if I was okay. I told him I was about to go home and was sleeping the last weeks away. He laughed and told me that if Popeck got to me I could come into his office to rant.

I wasn't singled out. He is like that with most people. The maddest I ever saw him was when I went in to help him with the paperwork on a new arrival. He was livid and cussing up a storm. The new lady was 92 and had been given a 10 year sentence for conspiracy. Before she arrived he went to the open bus stop that was to be her new home and made an announcement. He told them her age and that he expected them to treat her with respect. They would have anyway but this let them know that he was keeping an especially close eye on her.

The last time I saw him was the night before I left. I said goodbye and walked him to the door as he left for the day. He wished me well, gave me a pat on the back and sang "The Gambler" as he walked to his Jeep.

The Night Guard of the Year!

I debated on whether or not to include this. For anyone official that might read this: He had nothing to do with it and it wasn't his fault!

Disclaimer done, Robby Puckett was the 2010 Night Guard of the Year! For the few days leading up to his leaving, jokes were played on him and the last night, just before his relief came to take over, he was presented with a toilet seat with the above "2010 Night Guard of the Year" glittered on it. A few people had snuck out to his car with water and glitter. It was fun and Puckett is a great guy. He put up with a lot of nagging and bitching from us. He deserved the award.

Crook on the Hook

One of my favorite evening officers was Mr. Crook. For starters, you have to love a correctional officer with a name like "Crook." He really had only two choices in life and I'm glad he made the right one. He was great and keeping order and control by making us laugh.

The indomitable Mr. Weiss

My other favorite evening officer was Mr. Weiss. He was stoic, regal and had a wickedly dry sense of humor. He was also unfailing kind, thoughtful and caring. One of my favorite personal memories of him is seeing him in the hall and mentioning that I knew about his girlfriend. There was no one around or I would never have said it. Even a flip accusation can cause them grief. He knew me pretty well by then as I had been the tour guide for some time at this point but his eyes narrowed and he took a step back. I laughed and asked him when Angel would be moving in with him. Then he cracked up. Angel is the dog he adopted from the dog program and he doted on her from the moment they met. Anyone who treats a dog the way he treated her gets a mention in my book!

Because he was so seemingly stern, one of my penthouse roomies wanted to make him laugh. She would dress up in bizarre outfits and just stand there at count time. Then she started making up a comic routine. One night he broke. He just flat out lost it as he came in to count. Weiss was doubled over laughing when the second count officer arrived. The other officer stood back until it passed. The other officer asked what his number was at that point or if they needed to recount. Having heard his number as he approached the door, I whispered it to him and the count continued. We kept the jokes going with him after that. He would loudly announce his number as he approached the door just in case.

The greatest thing he did was stand up for us. As hot as it was in the summer, it was pretty cold in the winter. They didn't turn the heat on until November and it was cold all the time. People, myself included, started taking up crochet just to have an extra blanket. This was when they took our second blanket. Weiss wasn't terribly motivated to find our hidden blankets. In fact I have long suspected that he knew where we had them hidden. He actually went and complained about the living conditions at that point. One thin blanket was simply not enough in November. While all of the officers did everything they could to make things easier for us within the rules, Weiss was one of the few to take on the administration to try and help us. It must have worked because they turned on the heat early.

Living at Atwood Hall

Your Sentence and Crime

Few people will immediately ask you about your crime. They are more inclined to ask you how long you will be there. The information your sentence gives tells them far more than you might think.

There are no violent criminals in Atwood Hall or any other prison camp. There is a less than zero chance of a riot, fight, strike or any other maladaptive behavior. It simply does not happen at these camps.

The main charges of the women here are going to be drug use/manufacture, conspiracy, financial crimes and tax crimes. Everyone knows that the moment you arrive.

You are free to discuss your crime all you like. Keep in mind that there are government snitches here as well. Don't share information that the feds don't already know about.

As for the length of your sentence, well the general maximum sentence for someone in a camp is supposed to be 10 years. In theory no one gets sent to a camp if they have more than 10 years to serve. However the reality is that close to the end of my 15 months I gave a tour to a woman serving 12 years. So as with everything else you will hear, take the maximum length with a grain of salt.

If you are serving less than 3 years you don't want to spend a lot of time whining about it. It tends to irritate those with far longer sentences. Those of you reading this that will serve 3-6 months can expect very little sympathy about the length of their sentence.

Commissary Shopping

Most self-surrenders are on Tuesdays and Wednesdays. If you arrive with cash then the money should be on your commissary account by the following morning. If your money is sent to you via Western Union then it may be on there or you may have to wait until the following Tuesday to shop.

You are allowed to go to the commissary once a week. Shopping is Tuesday and Thursday. You can pick up a commissary list at the commissary window and if you are smart you will pick up a new one each time you shop. You put your name and inmate number on the top of the list and then look over the list and make your selections. There is a space next to each item on the list and you write in the number of that item that you want.

At the commissary window is a write on board that lists the new items as well as items that are out of stock. There is also a list for ice cream. It's not unusual for friends to double up on the ice cream by buying some for a friend on Tuesday and then the friend buying some for them on Thursday. It makes life more bearable to share, even in prison.

The official rules limit the number of certain items you can buy but this was never enforced. As a general rule if it fits into your locker you can have as much as you want. In the entire time I was there I never once heard of anyone getting into trouble for having a large number of commissary items stored in their locker. I knew one woman that had an entire locker full of Diet Mountain Dew. Mountain Dew wasn't hard to get but the diet version was rare so she had stocked up.

There are several shopping carts for when you buy a big load but if you can't get them you can always find a friend to help out. Especially if it's the one you treat to ice cream! The other option is to use your laundry bag. You take it back to your room and unload it. Please return the shopping cart as quickly as possible; other people need to use it.

One of your first purchases will be a mug. Without that and a water bottle there is no way to drink anything outside of mealtimes except at the water fountains. In an odd twist of fate the mugs are Taster's Choice mugs. You can't make this kind of crap up.

Food

There are two things you will notice immediately upon arrival: The obesity rate and the obsession with mealtimes. I actually lost a great deal of weight because I slept so much and because my best friends did as well. With the exception of strawberry frosted flakes and chocolate turnovers, I skipped breakfast. I always do at home and I preferred to sleep that extra hour.

Lunch is the dessert meal. Cookies, leftover turnovers and banana pudding are popular. I skipped lunch most of the time as well. Because Valarie, my best friend, worked out of the building, she had an early lunch. She would come and wake me if there was a good dessert or salad. Then I would eat. Our new unit manager pushed and got us more salads so I ate lunch a lot during my last few months. I always went to lunch on Wednesday. Wednesday is Hamburger Day. It's absolutely always Hamburger Day. Even if it's a holiday (then it was bacon burgers…thank you Mr. White!) Hamburgers, fries and cookies is the typical Wednesday lunch.

Dinner is immediately following the 4pm count. If there was salad for lunch then there will be the leftover salad for dinner. Taco nights were popular but nothing beat out chef salad night.

No matter what happens, there will be a line for food. You line up down the hall by the officer station. Oddly enough, you line up on one side for breakfast and lunch but on the other for dinner. When the cafeteria doors open you file in and pick up a tray, a cup and silverware. Then you go through the line. At the end of it you get a drink. Sometimes there is a station set up after the main line where extra leftovers from lunch, such as salad, are sitting and you can take as much as you can fit on your plate. When you finish eating you dump your tray. Don't loiter because the room can only hold about 50 people at a time and there are around 300 to serve.

The food isn't great and it isn't horrible. You will get used to it quickly and even look forward to some of it. I rather enjoyed the salads, taco nights and even the holiday meals. I think part of it was the information that filtered out about how the man in charge of food service as well as the officer that oversaw the meal shifts fought to get us decent meals. Camps are an afterthought and we are not treated with as much care and concern as the "real" prisons. That those in charge of us cared as much as they did made things better; even the food.

In the commissary you can buy food, condiments and other edibles. I urge you to try the caramel puffies, the green apple twizzlers and the buddy bars. I still eat those. I also developed a tasted for the sweet hot sauce which is great on just about everything and the honey mustard salad dressing. What is incredibly amazing is the food that can be made from the stuff in the commissary as well as a few things nicked from the kitchen.

Finally, you are not allowed to take food from the cafeteria to your rooms. When I first arrived we were able to take a piece of fruit with us to our rooms. Then there was a magnificent raid on the men next door and it was discovered that they have brewed up 50 gallons of booze. That was the end to our having fruit in our rooms; officially. We still sneak it out. They know we do it but pretend otherwise.

Rooms

There are no cells here. There are no bars on the windows and there are no locks on anything other than staff offices as far as I could tell. I once wandered outside at 2 in the morning. Oh, there are also no video cameras.

There is this widely held belief that everyone starts in the "Bus Stop" which is a large dorm room and has to earn a smaller room. The reality is that you will be put where they have space. I started in the Open Bus Stop which was once a day room but was converted into a large open dorm with no door. It could hold 25 without being cramped. I was moved into a closed room that held 8 about four months after I arrived. Then I was moved to the room on the 3rd floor known as The Penthouse. This was a large dorm room with 12 people but there was a huge windowed alcove with a table and chairs in it. I was there for 4 months before the 5-Star ended up with an open bed. I asked for it because it had a private bathroom. A woman will do a lot to only have to share a bathroom with two other people! There are many 2 and 3 bed rooms and it's considered a privilege to have one of those.

You and your roommates are responsible for cleaning your room. Contrary to television, you do not use sanitary napkins for this. There is plenty of cleaner and rags for you to use. Either ask an orderly for these things or ask Ms. Brown.

Beds

You will, of course, have a bed. Do not expect luxury here. It's a metal frame with springs and a mattress on top. Generally, if you are over 45 you get a bottom bunk. That is not etched in stone by any stretch of the imagination. I actually rather enjoyed my top bunk nestled into a corner.

Because the mattresses are covered in an anti-bacterial vinyl covering you will want to use your blanket on it in the summer. Cover it with one of your two sheets and use the other sheet as a cover. Trust me when I write that this will be all the cover you will need in the summer. There are also no fitted sheets. I was very lucky that Tasha showed me how to make flat sheets work. You tie knots in the corners of the sheets and then loop them into the springs; it works surprisingly well.

If you have a top bunk you also get possession of a chair. Some people get very possessive of their chairs. You should ask before sitting in it. This is also true of beds. Unless it's a close friend you should ask permission or wait until an offer to sit on the bed is made.

Bathing

If you watch enough prison movies or television shows then this will be something that has you greatly concerned. It seems that there is always at least one infamous shower scene that involves sex and/or a beating. Not in Atwood Hall. The shower situation is not all that bad. There are two large bathrooms on each of the second and third floors. There is one on the first floor. There are also 2 single person bathrooms on each of the second and third floors and one on the first floor.

Some people use the large shower rooms. In these rooms there is between 3 and 4 individual showers with a privacy curtain. These are usually faster to get into than the single person bathrooms. There is typically an invisible line to the single showers. It's invisible because no one usually waits in an actual line. They simply find out who is last in the line and say "I'm after you." When that person finishes they will call out your name and you go take your turn. There are no locks on the doors but the doors open inward and there is a convenient trashcan that can be used as a 'lock' of sorts. It was never a problem while I was there. After moving into the 5-star where we had our own bathroom I took showers at

3pm. My two roommates preferred 8pm and 7am so there was never an issue there either.

In the entire time I was at Atwood Hall the only naked person I ever saw was myself.

All soaps and shampoos are purchased in the commissary. Even hair dye is available there as well. You can either apply it yourself or have it done in the beauty shop.

It will likely come as something of a surprise to find that you can also buy razors in the commissary. They aren't great but they get the job done.

Laundry

Given the number of clothing items you have, you will need to do laundry at least once a week. Many of the campers here that have been to other camps have commented on the fact that here we have to provide our own laundry detergent. It seems that in many other camps it is provided for you. It is what it is and you will need to get some detergent from the commissary.

Every morning at about 6am the laundry sign-up sheet goes on the wall by the office. You need to sign up fast to get a slot. I never had to worry about this because I had friends that worked outside the building and they had to be up at that time. They would sign both of us up and I would do the laundry. There were other times when my duties as an orderly had me working in the various laundry rooms. At those times I would just do laundry while I worked. In theory, no one is supposed to do their laundry while we are working. Unless I was doing my own I would always let them go ahead and use the machines. 6 sets of machines and 300 women mean that the machines are almost always running.

You have the option of washing your bedding or taking it down to the unit laundry and changing it out for new stuff. I just did mine and didn't worry about being up in time for laundry exchange.

Window Shopping

You may think you know what that means but until you get to Atwood Hall you don't have a clue. Whenever someone is leaving, finished with a newspaper or book or just has stuff that they want to get out of their locker, they put it in one of the windows. Usually they put the stuff on the window sill by the door to the main staircase. It's yours for the taking!

Lockers

I was fixated on my locker. At one point when I had been sick for about a week, one of my roommates commented to no one in particular "she must be feeling better, she's playing with her locker again." My locker was always one of the cleanest and neatest in the building. There was a reason for this. You see while I wasn't hording commissary items I WAS stashing more books than the rules allowed. If the lockers should be examined I wanted it to be nothing more than a cursory glance and for there to be no need to carefully examine the number of books I had. I was more than a little paranoid about it.

I was very lucky in that all of my lockers had plenty of shelves. I managed to fold and keep my clothing on a single shelf. This is not as difficult as you might think; I had an expert teach me how to fold clothing so compact that I could fit 7 t-shirts into the space of a single shirt at home.

There were three times when my locker was 'searched.' The first was about 3 weeks after I arrived and Ms. Sloan was searching for contraband (garden produce.) As we were leaving the area so she could conduct the search I asked if she preferred my locker locked or unlocked. She looked at the open door, patted me on the back and told me to go ahead and lock it. It was never reopened.

The second time was when the warden had instructed the unit manager to remove our second blankets. He hated it but had no choice but to comply. He was also required to check our lockers to make sure we weren't hiding the now contraband second blanket. My locker was standing open and he glanced in it. Then he did a double take and stared at it. He asked who the locker belonged to and my roommates were silent. You don't rat out your roommates in prison. I volunteered that it was mine and he said it was the neatest locker he had ever seen. He then left without giving much of a glance to the other lockers in the room. We then went to the hiding place for the blankets and all was well. On the off chance someone in authority should read this I'll not mention the hiding place. Trust me when I say that your roommates can tell you.

The third time was when there was a new edict that required a nightly room search. The poor evening officer had to search at least one room per night. This was pointless and everyone knew it. The room I was in at this point was small and had only 3 of us. One woman that was so religious that everyone, myself included, could barely tolerate her presence when she was awake. The other was a 78-year-old Jewish woman that was hell on wheels. The officer was tired and I was the only person in the room at the time so instead of having me leave (the official procedure) he sat down in a chair and asked me if I had any contraband. My locker was partially open and I looked towards it. He glanced at it and said, "Guess not" and then sat talking to me during the rest of the allotted search time.

The point here is that your locker is subject to being searched but in Lexington searches are very rare and unless you are doing something stupid then you will have nothing to worry about. While I was there the top contraband items were:

- Food from the kitchen
- Produce from the garden
- Cigarettes

The only times I heard of something more illicit was when some idiot tried to smuggle in marijuana. It never actually made it to the camp as it was found when she was being processed and she was immediately removed to the county jail. She never made it back to the camp. While I don't know for certain, it's probable that she was met with new charges and sent to an actual prison.

Bulletin Boards

Everyone wants a board. I was really incredibly lucky in that a woman left about 10 days after I arrived and she gave me her board. You hang it on the wall by your bed and you keep pictures on it. I also kept a small 12 month calendar on it. Because my sentence was 18 months I had printed a calendar on card stock before I left home. One year for each side. It was in the first package I had sent to me. It is really very satisfying to mark off each day.

Mostly, you will keep photos of family and friends on it. You can "introduce" your new friends to your pets, family and friends through this.
Psychologically, it's nice to have them close. Like many, I would touch each photo before I went to bed at night. Yes, I know it seems sad but it is what it is. You do whatever is necessary to get through it.

Team Meetings

In theory you will have your first Team Meeting within 30 days of your arrival. It took the powers that be 45 days to get around to having mine. The meeting took all of about 2 minutes so don't get comfortable in the chair.
Roughly every 3 months after that you have another Team Meeting and it's the same thing every time. The team is made up of your counselor, your case manager and the unit manager. They have an update from your boss, discuss your programming and send you on your way. About a week before the meeting you will be sent an in-house memo that asks you to list what you have been doing since your last team meeting. Obviously, on the first one you will specify that you have just arrived.

Programming

You are going to be told how incredibly important this aspect of your time in Lexington (and other camps) is to things like half-way house time and your eventual release. Let me blow a few myths out of the water for you right now:

Programming has absolutely nothing at all to do with your good-time credit. Taking a lot of classes will not get you out of prison one day sooner. Taking nothing will not keep you one day longer. It will have no impact on your treatment in Lexington and it doesn't impact what rooms you get. Programming has absolutely no impact on your life in Lexington at all.

The majority of programming in Lexington focuses on things such as childhood trauma, drug and alcohol use or parenting. There were a few other classes for things that were supposed to be helping you to find a career after you were released.

You will get the form I mentioned and after the first team meeting you are supposed to list what parts of your programming you have completed. I have never been very good at being dictated to by people who know less about me than a stranger on the street. I had a lot of fun with these.

I know people that went over their team reports and sent cop-outs to get into every class that they were told to take. Then there was me. I didn't take anything listed on my team report. Ever.

I was put into the 'coping class' immediately upon arrival because, get this, I didn't like being there. Apparently I wasn't appreciative enough so the powers that be stuck me in this class. I attended twice. The first time I made it clear that I was not happy being there, had a far better life at home and was counting down the weeks until I could leave. The psychologist was unaware that I had never been in prison before or that I was only there for a few months. The second time I made it clear that I wouldn't be back. I was never again on the call-out sheet for 'coping class' so I do have a measure of respect and affection for the psychologist for respecting my decision.

As for programming, I didn't take any of it and it drove my case manager nuts. At my third team meeting she asked me why I hadn't taken any classes. I told her I didn't want to take them. She then made the mistake of informing me that she was a professional and was assigning me those classes because she felt it was what was best for me. She then looked at me and said, "Why do you think they are paying me?!" I looked her right in the eye and informed her that I didn't know why she was being paid and that it was clear that she knew nothing about my case, what I needed or me. I told her that making someone who never drank alcohol take a class about alcohol abuse was asinine. At that point the unit manager piped up that it was also for the use of other illegal drugs. Before I would respond, my counselor, Ms. Brown pointed out that I didn't have a drug history either. Ms. Brown then signed my papers and told me I could go. My team meetings were much smoother after that.

I kept a list of the things I put on my self-reporting paper about what I had been doing with my time in Lexington. Here is that list:
- Reading books
- Reading the Bible
- Teaching Russian
- Studying the theory M3
- Waiting for the Mother ship

- Cleaning my locker
- Showing new people around
- Contemplating my place in the Grand Design
- Allowing for cellular regeneration in an efficient manner (napping....they didn't get it either)

It was funny that the case manager eventually seemed to admire my defiance. By the time I left, Ms. Miller and I were getting along great.

Education

You know those stories of inmates getting law degrees in prison? Yeah, that doesn't happen here. Education here has only one single focus and that is for you to get your GED. If you graduated High School then there is nothing much here for you. If you didn't, then you are required to attend classes and get your GED.

For people with longer sentences that have a GED or graduated High School there is a dental hygiene program and there is a Braille program. Both are small classes, hard to get into and unless you have 3 or more years you will not even be considered. If you have a college degree of any kind there is nothing in the education department for you.

Computers

When I left there were 6 of them on the second floor. You can use these to check your inmate account balance, add money to your phone account and send email. All email is subject to being read, just like your regular mail. It IS read. I know three people who got into trouble over what was in their email. You have to set up each email address and it is verified by the system before you can send or receive email. All of the email is held within a closed system. They have to log into an email account that they set up on the correctional system email portal. You can only send and receive email through this portal. There is no other Internet access. You are charged a set rate while you are on the computer. I helped out slow-typing friends frequently by typing lengthy messages for them in a fraction of the time it would have cost them. Time is money here people!

Telephones

These are located on the main floor, around the corner from the medical unit and the chapel. There were 5 phones and they were almost always in use. You get a set amount of time each month for phone call with most months being at 300 minutes and November and December being 400 minutes. You can use these in 15-minute increments. After the 15 minutes is up you have to wait until the system resets which is normally after an hour. The cost per minute is around $0.25. I didn't use all of mine. Phone minutes are expensive. These calls are monitored.

You can only make calls. There is no way for them to call you. When you make the call they will have to accept it by pressing a number on their phone. It will tell the person on the other end that they are getting a call from a prison. Then, in case either of you forget, every 2 or 3 minutes it will remind you both that the call is from a prison. Oddly enough, you never get used to this.

Religion

For all the talk about the separation of church and state, the removal of religion from the public square and the atheists running amok, religion is alive and well in prison. While special provisions will be made for chapel time for Jews and Muslims, Christianity is everywhere. I mean that as literally as I possibly can. The officers, the counselors, the doctor are all constantly invoking God. This didn't bother me as much as it surprised me. There are Bible verses on the bulletin boards in the hall, people are constantly praying in the halls and there are enough Bible classes to fill your time. They have "outreach" workers and preachers in almost every night giving motivational talks. One of them taught people how to get a hotel room upgrade by telling the desk that you saw a roach. It's amazing the things you learn in prison.

One afternoon I was waiting with a friend in the pill line when Dr. Clancy walked past. He turned around immediately and started back to his office, obviously having forgotten something. The Popeck, who didn't like Dr. Clancy, blurted out "Are you lost?" Without missing a beat he replied, "I was but then I found Jesus!"

When I became the tour guide I also started collecting Bibles from those going home. Part of the tour was to show the new ladies the chapel and I would always ask them if they wanted a Bible. No one ever said no. It was also possible to have one sent to you for free. The list of places that will send them is on the wall in the religion library.

There is a list of services on the door to the chapel. Check for one that suits your needs. You will want to get there early because attending church is very popular.

If you are not a Christian my advice here is to simply keep it to yourself. This is not an environment where you want to rock the boat and the staff is largely evangelical. If you have issues with how overt the religious display is then save it until you get home. It really isn't worth it to cause problems of that nature.

Healthcare

Much has been made about the horrible healthcare in prisons. I didn't see that here as I mentioned earlier. Of course I was not parked on the bench outside the office every day either.

If you are sick, head down for sick call at 7:30 in the morning. If you get sick later in the day you can wander over to the office if necessary.

Many medications are self-administered. The Prozac they gave me was kept in my locker. Other drugs require you to get into the pill line in the morning and afternoon.

To get a refill on self-administered meds you drop the wrapper of the bottle into the pill box on the wall. Then in the afternoon you get into the pill line and pick them up.

If you need to see the dentist or psychologist fill out a cop out form and drop it into the mail box. If you need a Prozac adjustment you can send a cop-out form for that as well.

Shots

A shot is what it's called when you get into trouble and receive a disciplinary note. That is pretty much all I know about them because not only did I never get one I only know a couple of people who did. They mostly ended up spending a few days at county and then came back. A couple of people made mistakes big enough that they didn't come back. Common sense works well to avoid getting a shot. Don't do anything stupid, don't argue with the officers and you will be fine. It's not difficult to avoid getting a shot.

Just in case you think it's bad being in prison, if you get a shot that merits an even more insane time out than you are already serving, you get to go to county! That's right ladies; if you are naughty you will go and spend some time at the local county jail. I'm still trying to work out how this is a bad thing in and of itself. You see fed inmates are housed by themselves. They have their own television, their meals are brought to them and they don't have to work. Oh, it's also air conditioned. Still, it's not a good idea to be seen as a troublemaker.

Cop-Outs

You can get the forms at the office. This is a one sheet form that you send to an officer or other staff member. After you fill it out you drop it into the mail box. If you have a toothache and need to see the dentist then you will send her a cop-out form. In a few days, depending on the issue, you will be on the call-out sheet for an appointment. You can also request room assignments and change jobs by submitting a cop-out form.

Money and Finances

You are allowed to spend $320 a month in the commissary. Any medications you buy, stamps and phone time will not count against this amount. In December that amount goes to $370. You can also buy shoes, yarn and other special items.

The easiest and cheapest way to have money added to your account is to have a family member send it via Western Union. You need to understand before you leave home that you are responsible for buying all you necessities such as soap, laundry detergent, shampoo, aspirin and so forth while you are in prison. You must purchase your own lock for your locker as well as a radio. This is very hard to do if you are relying on only your monthly pay for income.

The other financial aspect of prison life is that you will be assessed any fines or fees. Almost everyone is hit with an assessment fee of $100. The average 6 month balance of your account is how your payment is determined. This calculation starts on the first calendar month after you arrive. It's one of the few things that they do right. You have most of your expenses the first month as you purchase you leisure clothing, lock, fan and radio.

Any restitution that you have to pay will start being charged after your release. You do not have to begin paying on it while you are in custody.

Inmate ID

While you are at R&D, immediately upon arrival, you will be issued your ID card. It has your inmate number on it along with a photo. In some camps you need to keep this with you, apparently. Atwood Hall never required that. You will need the number to make phone calls, log into the computer and several other functions. You will also need it at the Commissary and you should take it with you if you need any medical services.

Race Issues

The day after I arrived I was sitting outside in the pavilion when a very nice black woman asked me to join her on her walk. I had the haunted look that I came to recognize in new people. As we were walking she asked me if I had a problem with black folks. I thought it was an odd question considering I was walking with her. I told her I didn't and she told me that I would before I left. She was right.

Before arriving at Atwood Hall I didn't much notice race. People were people. I'm much more guarded now. To be fair, the vast majority of black ladies I met were really great people. Tasha was a doll; there was Fluffy who was a sweetheart and wise Flora just to name a few. Then there was Shawna. She and I became fast friends. The problem is that there is a great deal of racism and segregation here and it's all from the black ladies that have chips on their shoulders. They were the troublemakers and the thieves.
Shawna hadn't been there a full day before Butters demanded to know why she was talking to me. Black girls were not allowed to be friends with white girls (or Hispanic girls or Asian girls...etc.)

They were also not allowed to "act white" which apparently means that they aren't allowed to use proper grammar, have an education and read something other than porn.

Oddly enough there were no other issues. All of the other groups got along fine. No one had a problem with the black girls but they had a problem with everyone else. As I said, it wasn't all of them. It was enough of them though to put you on your guard. Thankfully one of the worst got into serious trouble stealing and ended up getting sent to a real prison with a new sentence. It's apparently a lot quieter there now.

If you are black and reading this, please don't fall into that trap. There are plenty of nice people in Atwood Hall. Segregating yourself and getting involved with troublemakers and racists like that will only bring you down. You are better than that.

Sex

To quote Tussey "Stay away from that lesbian shit!" Here is the reality of sex at Atwood Hall: It happens. It's there. Deal with this fact and move on. It will not be constant, it will not be overt and it will not be forced. I talked to a lot of people before I left specifically because I knew I would write this book. Not one person had ever heard of any type of sexual abuse at Atwood Hall or any other camp. As laid back and relaxed as this place is you can be certain that it would not be tolerated for a minute.

Technically, sex is forbidden. So if you do it, don't get caught. If someone is pressuring you to do something you don't want to do, send a cop-out to the psychologist, one of the officers or the unit manager. They will put a stop to it immediately.

Hygiene and Toilet Paper

One of the weirdest things I had to get used to doing was carting toilet paper with me to the bathroom. At least it's free. You are given two rolls a week. There are no toilet paper holders in the bathrooms so you take the toilet paper with you. It's weird. I got lucky and most of my stay here I was in the 5-star. It had a bathroom and a toilet paper holder.

Tampons and sanitary napkins are also provided. You pick them up when you get the toilet paper.

Here is how it works: You will be going merrily along with your day and suddenly someone will shout "Toilet Paper" and everyone will run to where the line is forming. Sometimes they just give it to you and you leave. Other times they give it to you and check your name off a list. Either way, you must stop whatever you are doing and get in that line.

Mail

This is huge. Mail is probably the single biggest deal all day. There is nothing more valued than a letter or package from home. I have a wonderful friend that would send me packages of paperback books, puzzle books and newspaper clippings. It was wonderful and everyone in the place would ask me what Jane had sent. They knew who she was because of the packages.

Hardback books must be sent from the publisher and I had actually pre-ordered a number of books from Amazon to have delivered to me while I was in Lexington. Friends sent books for Christmas and my Birthday this way as well.

Every weeknight at about 5:45 the mail list would be posted to the wall by the office. Everyone would gather around to check for their name. I was designated by my room and a friend that didn't get much mail to check for their names as well as my own. If you have mail, you can pick it up at 6pm or the second call at 8pm. You stand in the lobby and wait for your name to be called. Then you take your mail and share with your friends. I have wonderful memories of curling up on the bunk with Valarie while we went through a Jane Package while sharing buddy bars and soda. We would each pick a new book to start and hang out. I left all of those books there.

Because it can apparently be a mechanism for drug smuggling, your family cannot send you stamps. They also cannot send you money. Any money they wish to send must be sent to your inmate trust account. Those are the rules. Because your mail is searched it will be found and the offending items returned to sender. That doesn't always happen though. Jane was able to send me highlighters and highlighter pencils. Sometimes they got through….sometimes they didn't She just kept sending them until they slipped through. One notable day I got a letter from my oldest kid and it contained stamps and a $20 bill. I was beside myself, thinking I was about to be in really serious trouble. I quickly put the money in an envelope and sent it home. The poor kid was in tears on the phone worried that I had to go to the "hole." I never laughed as hard as I did after that conversation. There is no hole there and I doubt anyone would have cared even if they had found the money. I kept the stamps.

Smoking

Here is an interesting problem: On the front door and next to the visitor entrance there are signs warning visitors that bringing contraband into a Federal prison is a felony. Yet every day several staff members bring their tobacco into the building. Smoking by inmates is strictly forbidden. It's an automatic trip to county if it's even suspected. While I was there cigarettes were often in the mix. I chose to not smoke the entire time I was there and foolishly started again on the way home. A dead giveaway that someone has been smoking is when she comes out of the shower and her best friend gives her a prolonged hug. That person is smelling her to make she the smoke smell is gone.

I'm not going to name names here but one officer caught two different friends of mine smoking. One went to county and one didn't. The one who went to county lied to the officer and it pissed him off. Had she been honest with him, as my other friend was, he would have let it go the first time and just issued a stern warning.

I highly recommend giving up smoking completely. They really aren't worth the trouble that you can get into and you will be healthier for it.

Ice Machines

There are two industrial ice machines outside of food service. They are located on the second floor and the first floor. There are between 300 and 320 women in the camp at a time. There is no air conditioning.

Just for good measure, Sloan would padlock the machines closed from 7 in the morning until 4 in the afternoon in the summer. I'm still really pissed off about that. It was between 100 and 115 degrees in the building during the day. The record was 125 degrees. Two machines full of ice and they were padlocked shut. On a more positive note, Sloan mostly stayed in her air conditioned office during the summer so we rarely had to deal with her during the worst of the heat.

Several times friends that worked in food service would bring up bags filled with ice. One of my friends was an early riser and would get me a cup of ice before it was cut off. Years later I can't begin to tell you how much that meant to me. It was an unbelievable gift.

Thankfully there doesn't seem to be any padlocks on the ice machines these days. Sloan retired and I guess she took her padlocks with her.

Recreation and Fitness

There is a popular misconception that federal prisons have incredible gyms, swimming pools and all sorts of recreation programs. This doesn't exist here and I never heard of it existing anywhere else in the real world.

What you get here is a small basement gym with old machines. It's very small but it is quite popular in the summer because it is air conditioned. There is also an outdoor walking area. It's just a road to one of the community buildings on the property but people walk it constantly. A rather large number of people clocked enough miles to have walked home.

We had a recreation officer for a while when I first arrived. He had so little success and there were so many complaints that he eventually quit trying. The offerings he suggested were lame attempts at getting us up to walk or visit the gym. He thought that banging on our lockers to wake us up would be motivational. It wasn't and he was told to stop doing that.

The real recreation programs here are inmate led. We have had line dancing, aerobics, yoga and so forth. There was a bean bag toss deal for a while and I actually participated in that. I didn't want to but Valarie did and she needed a partner.

Visitations

A 10 hour drive and only 15 months prevented me from having any visits when I was in camping at Atwood Hall. Many of my friends had frequent visits. One older lady would get monthly visits from her husband who lived in Florida. We loved him and as he needed to use the elevator to get to the visitation room, we always greeted him warmly. The same was true of friends who had small children. As long as the officers know that you aren't up to something they will be pretty lax.

Visits take place on Friday afternoons and Saturdays. For the inmate, you have to wear your greens and take your ID. You spend time in the indoor air conditioned visitation room or in the outside visiting area. There are snack machines for your family and sharing is allowed.

Drug Testing

I was never tested but it does happen every now and then. It's not a big deal. When they got a breathalyzer and I had never seen one I offered to test it out and told them to just put my name on the list if they wanted. When you have no history of drug or alcohol use you never get on the list.

A few hours later my name was on a list by the office door. I went to see what the officer wanted and he said "I need you to blow me." He immediately realized what he said, didn't say another word and handed me the machine. I knew what he meant to say so I blew, was negative and told him to have a nice night.

The next day Tussey popped by my room and asked me about the incident. The officer had told him about it and was worried about me. I told Tussey it was no big deal, I understood what was intended and took it that way. Later that night when the officer was back on duty I went and told him not to worry that I wasn't going to report him for saying something inappropriate. It turns out that he was worried that he had frightened me and wanted to make sure I was okay. He's a nice guy and pretty typical of the officers there.

The Men's Facility

This bears only a brief mention. You may find that on occasion you need to go over to "A" building which is the men's facility. There is a lot of security there because they do have high-security inmates in the medical area. You will not see them. Please don't try.

During the tour one of the things pointed out to me and one of the things I later mentioned to the ladies I took on the tour was to not be stupid. There have been instances of people throwing notes and packages to the men and even flashing them. Considering the distance involved it's impressive, to say the least, that anyone can throw anything that far. As for the flashing, well you would have to use your imagination. Getting caught on the other hand would be a very bad thing. I can promise you a shot, extra duty and probably a trip to county for that.

Holidays

Atwood Hall runs on a weekend schedule during all holidays. That means brunch and then a holiday dinner. The meals are actually pretty nice thanks to the officers. You can expect the traditional foods and a long line. Breaking with the normal rules, they generally allow you to take your food out of the cafeteria. Some take it to the tables outside and many return to their rooms with it.

Christmas was just plain weird. There is a huge turnover rate at the camps and by the time Christmas came along I was one of those who had been there the longest. Ms. Sloan became irritated that we had done no decorating. In hindsight she actually helped us a lot. We would have been sad and depressed without her prodding us to decorate the facility. It was really quite lovely with paper snowflakes all over the place and decorated Christmas trees.

A few days before Christmas we all had to go line up and get our Christmas bags from the facility. It sounds bizarre but it was a large bag filled with all sorts of treats. From candy bars to donuts to potato chips there were plenty of snacks in it. It wasn't as good as being at home but it was nice to get something and treats are always welcome.

The Dog Program

As a pet lover I found that one of the best parts of being here was that there were dogs and cats. The cats are strays that the inmates feed. The dogs are part of a second chance program. These are dogs that have been living in shelters and need socializing. There is one dog to each 4 person room. After the dog has been there a week those not in the program are allowed to pet and play with it.

To get into the dog program you have to have at least 2 years left on your sentence and getting in is tough. Ms. Miller has long been in charge of it and it's great for both inmates and dogs.

Pre-Release Classes

There is a rumor that you have to take 4 of these to be released. I took 2 even though my paperwork says I took 4. When you do as little as I did for 15 months you remember that sort of thing.

I took my first class less than 2 months after I arrived. It was about acclimating to life on the outside. I pointed out that I had not yet acclimated to life on the inside and I could go home and we could call it even. They didn't agree with me.

My second class was on being in a half-way house and supervised release. The entire point was to scare the hell out of people in regards to the release officer and to prevent us from braiding the hair of the opposite sex and playing basketball with them. I still have no idea what that means. Everything else was a lie. I should point out that I never had the opportunity to either play basketball or braid hair while I was in the half-way house. Go figure.

Going Home

When I would give new people their tour I always pointed out to them that a place with a travel agent couldn't be all bad! The happiest day you will spend in Atwood Hall is the day you go and see the Travel Agent to get your orders to go home. There are a few things you need to know about this however.

For starters, you are not allowed to tell people what your actual itinerary is going to be. They really do mean this and I saw more than one person lose her half-way house time because she discussed it on the phone. In one very tragic case, the woman lost her mother about a week later. Instead of seeing her one last time she was sitting in her room. You can send it out in a letter but you will be at the half-way house before the letter arrives. They don't give you a lot of notice. If you are being picked up by a family member then you can inform them of what time to be there to get you.
If you go via bus you have more flex time to get to the half-way house. If you go with your family you have almost no margin for emergencies.

You also need to realize that if you are going to a half-way house then you are still an inmate in federal custody.

The scariest night you will spend in Atwood Hall is 2 days before your release. You will not relax until you are on the call-out sheet for the merry-go-round (MGR.) This is aptly named because there is nothing merrier than going around and getting the various staff members to sign you out. You will leave the following day.

Your release morning will be busy with you turning in your greens, bedding, and saying good-bye to your friends.

You can take your personal belongings with you but please note that if you are going via bus then you will have to haul the box around from stop to stop. It's much better to travel light or mail stuff home.

As soon as I got to my first layover I phoned home. I made arrangements and asked my husband to let the other family members know what was going on with me.

I had a 3-hour layover in the city where my oldest works. She surprised me with a visit and brought along her 2-year old son. As she hugged me for the first time in over a year she asked "Where are they?" She was referring to my guards. I found out later that she had asked my husband if the guards would let her talk to me. That must have been a daunting trip for her yet she made it anyway. She thought I would be in an orange jumpsuit, shackled and under armed guard. Instead I was wearing grey sweatpants, tennis shoes and traveling solo.

If you have a straight release to your home then you can take all the time you want. If you are going to a half-way house then you need to get there on time. If you are going to be late then you need to call. The half-way house may have issues with it but all they can do is report it to the Marshal Service. Your status as a camper makes you a very low priority.

Halfway Houses

The biggest lie I was ever told was by my attorney and it was long before sentencing. That lie was this: because I was a one-time offender I would probably only do about 4 months and then spend the rest of the time at a halfway house. When I found out that she was wrong, I was furious. I'm now quite grateful.

Next to your release date, everyone wants her halfway house date. Because of the length of my sentence (18 months) I was only to be given 2-4 months. At the time it was recommended, Ms. Miller and I were at odds and she recommended no halfway house time. The Unit Manager intervened and got me 2 months.

You have the right to refuse halfway house time; you can complete your entire sentence in Lexington. If my halfway house time had been during the winter I would have stayed put. My halfway house months were July and August and the halfway house was air conditioned so I left Lexington. I should have stayed.

Lexington has its faults but it's not a terrible place. It's horribly hot in the summer but it's survivable. The halfway house was horrible on a level that only someone who has been to prison can fully understand. It was the worst and longest two months of the entire ordeal.

All halfway houses are privately owned and under contract with the Federal government. To that end, they are all run in an almost identical manner. I will give them some leeway because they are required to transition all levels of Federal inmates, from camps to maximum security. You will be treated as though you had just come from a maximum-security institution. Let that sink in before you move on: You WILL be treated exactly the same as if you had been in a maximum security prison.

The place was clean and had air conditioning. The food was fine and you could smoke. Beyond that it was the most restrictive environment I have ever been in and the only time I felt dehumanized. There are weekly drug tests, random room searches, and constant pat-downs and breathalyzer tests.

Let me explain what I mean by constant. Go to breakfast; get patted down on your return. Step outside the door to get a soda from the machine, you will be subject to a breathalyzer and pat down. Go to a required for everyone class and get patted down on your return. Keep in mind that you are ALWAYS on camera. Ok, you aren't on camera in the bathroom. But you are everyplace else and I'm not 100% sure about the bathroom. It was never ending. I petitioned to avoid the weekly urine tests and was initially denied until I pointed out that the judge in my case had exempted me from it. They actually double-checked that it wasn't a mistake in the documentation. No one there believed that I wasn't subject to the same conditions in Lexington so I made them call. They were stunned to find out that I was telling the truth but it didn't change anything except reduce me from weekly to monthly urine tests. By the way, if you refuse the test you are automatically considered to be dirty....so much for innocent until proven guilty.

The halfway house claims that they want you to find a job. The truth is that they want you working a minimum wage fast food job that makes you easy to track. I had a career I would immediately step back into. It required using a computer and the Internet. This was a huge issue for them. I even offered to leave my netbook in the office and use it only at the library. Nope. Oh, I could go to the library. I could even access the Internet on the library computer. I just couldn't work on my own computer. No explanation was given to me. So I didn't work. I just sat and did nothing for two months. They were two very long and very boring months.

You will be required to take their classes at least 3 nights a week. This isn't a huge problem because there is nothing else to do. So I went and was bored. You need to understand the mentality at work here. When you don't fit their preconceived notion of an inmate then they don't quite know what to do with you so they tend to just leave you alone. The facilities stress that they are going to treat each person as an individual but they never did. Not even once. However they get incredibly upset when you point this out to them.

To their way of thinking, all inmates have drug and alcohol problems. We all come from abusive homes and abusive partners. None of us have educations or careers. For them the end all and be all is that they are going to teach us life skills such as how to get a job at McDonald's and that being hit by our partners is unacceptable. When they encounter someone that has no substance abuse issues, no abuse issues, a stellar education with the resulting career to go with it, they are left completely off balance. That makes them angry.

I did have some fun debating moments such as when the moron running the education class decided to deride me for not getting a GED in Lexington and for obviously thinking that I didn't need one. She even got the class involved in it. When she asked if she had gotten through to me I pointed out to her that I had more degrees than she did and would be happy to hold my university transcripts up against hers any day of the week. She never spoke to me again but she did report my "non-compliant behavior" to the staff psychologist. He thought it was hysterically funny.

The other class leader and I had a similar discussion over alcohol. He was explaining that as alcoholics we could never go to a bar. I was looking bored and he asked what I thought would happen if I went to a bar. I told him 'nothing' and he pointed out that I would think that but then I would go and decide that I could have a single drink and be fine. That would lead to a relapse. I pointed out to him that this was unlikely as I wasn't an alcoholic or a drug user and that if I went to a bar I'd get a soda the way I always had. He was nice about it and laughed. After that though, he just ignored me in the class.

If it sounds like I have resentment and animosity towards them it's because I do. The treatment we all received there was far more degrading than anything that happened in Atwood Hall. Consider that before you agree to your half-way house time. It really wasn't worth it for me.

As much animosity I have for the halfway house I want to point out that the basic staff members were great. It was the policies that they were forced to follow that were the problem. They were on camera every bit as much as we were, maybe more. Their jobs depended on it. I was given more than one apology by the staff members while I was there and when I came down with a bad cold the cooking staff even offered to make me some soup instead of the regular meal. These people were fine. It was the people in charge of the place and the classes that were jerks.

Here is the bottom line on these places: They are huge scams that are in it for the money, they do not give a damn about you and they get paid either way. If you don't toe the line you will be sent back to Atwood Hall. Depending on how much time you have in the half-way house, you might be willing to go. For the record, the most common reasons for being shipped back include drug or alcohol use, cell phone use, and getting pregnant by another inmate at the half-way house. The last one is my personal favorite. It happened more than you could possibly imagine.

Supervised Release

Given the number of people that returned to Atwood Hall for violation of their supervised release I'm either the luckiest person on earth or they were just really stupid people. I had two release officers. The first handed me over to the last one about a month after my release. I think, based on horror stories I have heard, that I just lucked into two really great people. I was low priority and I did nothing to make them focus on me.

When you are on supervised release you can only travel within a specified area unless you get permission, you have to get a job or have someone else support you, fill out monthly reports and stay out of trouble.

My first request to travel out of the area was almost immediate due to a family wedding that was 20 miles beyond my allowed area. It was granted until I pointed out that I didn't actually want to go. She laughed and told me to blame her. The reality, for me and other former campers, is that the rules are in place for other types of offenders. We can generally call in a request for travel or just go and note it on our forms. That last part will depend entirely on the type of officer you have.

I was worried about the new guy, Jay, until I met him. He is a lot like Tussey. At the end of my supervised release he stopped by the house to tell me I was being paperworked out. We chatted for a while. He's a really nice guy. I never had a problem with him and I think I only actually saw him 4 times in three years and that was because he was in the area and dropping off more monthly forms for me to send in to him. It was just never really an issue. Because we live in a small area he asked if we should run into each other someplace if I would prefer him to ignore me or if it was okay for him to say "hello." I told him I had no problem seeing him in public.

Many supervised release officers will not allow you to have contact with other inmates, felons or even post on websites like prisontalk.com. Mine was not only okay with it he encouraged it. My friends are drug offenders and I am not. I have absolutely no history of drugs and because of that I make for a good role model for those with that in their history.

My most notable interaction with Jay was when I found out that I wasn't going to be allowed to vote because I had been removed from the list and they wouldn't allow me to register. He made a phone call and fixed it.

Take what you hear in Atwood Hall with a grain of salt and hope for the best with your release officer. He or she will let you know what they expect. Treat them with honesty and respect and you will most likely get the same in return. They have huge caseloads of real criminals. Campers are low priority here and they spend their time and energy on those who are a real threat to society.

Prison is a Weird Place

Rehab or Prison

Being here is a great deal like being in an extremely generic rehab where the patient was never actually diagnosed but rather deemed in need of rehab by virtue of their arrival at the facility. Instead of a program designed to meet individual needs those here are considered to be in need of the most basic of life skills and education. It follows then that for those not in need of these things that not only is the entire process futile but it is often insulting. Someone with advanced degrees or even a high school education is seen as a mystifying creature. There are no programs in this place for those people and there is no attempt at using the knowledge and skills that these people possess beyond walking and crochet classes. Despite the number of people who are multi-lingual there exist no language classes beyond informal groups. Reading, watching television, walking and crochet are the primary recreational activities. GED and anti-drug classes are the primary educational activities. For those not interested in or lacking these skills, boredom is the chief danger. This is not a prison but rather a rehab run by morons.

Saran Wrap

When you are in a building with 300 women you are going to come into the most amazing diet attempts that you will ever see. One of the most popular is to spread hemorrhoid ointment all over your body and then wrap yourself in saran wrap. This doesn't work. It's also not allowed because to get the saran wrap you have to steal it from the kitchen.

One nutcase who called herself Pam was a big believer in the saran wrap method. She kept getting caught and getting bounced back to the bus stop for it. This happened a lot. 5 times in the month I knew her. I swear the woman was obsessed with wrapping herself up in saran wrap. If we couldn't find her for 10 minutes straight then she was probable wrapping herself up. Consider that I knew her in June and July, the hottest months, and you have to wonder just how mentally unbalanced she really was.

The Popeck

Of all the people I met in Atwood Hall, The Popeck stands out the most. At 78, Popeck was the only Jewish woman in the place. She was a stickler about getting her holidays off, getting her Sabbath time in the Chapel and eating pork chops. She really loved pork chops! I used to trade my pork chops for her salad. She was also obsessed with dying her hair and it was a striped combination of brown and blonde. I adored her.

She was in for bankruptcy fraud and once quipped that you should never wear a diamond Cartier watch to your bankruptcy meeting. She also arrived at the facility with 5 massive Louis Vuitton bags. Those were immediately shipped home.

For someone of her age you would have expected her to be the quiet grandmotherly type. You would be wrong. The closest thing I ever saw to a fight was one she started against a 25 year old. I drug her off to her room while the friends of the other girl attended to her. While this was going on The Popeck was screaming obscenities at the girl. The Popeck was a pip.

Very few people liked her because she could be so damn difficult. I could see through her but most people didn't bother. They just hated her and moved on with their lives. I explained to her case manager that the problem was that she was an old woman who was scared and that caused her to lash out. I don't know if that helped her at all during her final few months there but I hope it did. My last night there she had a cake made for me. It was really sweet.

She was a little woman and spent most of her time at Atwood in one kind of trouble or another. She was constantly getting shipped off to county. It wasn't until we became roommates and bunkmates that I would intervene. We had some arguments but I really did like her a lot. I still do. She's in her 80's and I'm sure still causing trouble.

Over the Moon

There are some big women here. I mean absolutely huge. They are lovely people but I never realized humans could get that big. One of those was named Terri. I liked her and she was great. The Popeck didn't like her and was constantly making comments about her weight. One day as we were in line for dinner Popeck made a rude comment and Terri had had enough. She turned around, dropped her pants and mooned her. Popeck was stunned.

Everyone else laughed. It happened about 10 days before I left and Tussey pulled me aside and sked if it was true. He could hardly contain himself. Without giving him the name of the mooner I told him it was true. He thought it was great. The Popeck had given him a lot of trouble.

Wearing of the Greens

This was one of the finest moments of The Popeck. When you have to get meds from the pill line you are required, more or less, to wear your greens and bring your ID. This is especially true if you are The Popeck. She went down without them. The nurse sent her back to our room. Rather than put on her greens, as any normal and reasonable person would have done, she just tucked the pants into the front of her shorts. This didn't fool the nurse who insisted she put them on before getting her pills. So right there in the hall The Popeck took off her shorts and pulled on her greens!

Two Lockers

You get one locker. If you have more stuff than can be contained in one locker then you need to get rid of some stuff. The Popeck didn't let a little thing like this stop her.

The Popeck was moved into the open bus stop after one of her many trips to county. The bed next to hers was vacant and thus there was an extra locker. The Popeck appropriated this locker and filled it with stuff. Someone in the Bus Stop told on her and the locker was raided. She would have been given until the next day to remove the stuff herself except she had to fly into a rage and piss off Tussey. She cussed, insulted and threw an adult version of a temper tantrum. She was hauled off to county again. I was told that the contents of her second locker would be dumped and her other locker would be packed out. Both were open so a couple of friends helped me to remove the food stuff and then combine all the other stuff into the one locker. We made a list of the food stuff in case she came back. She did but didn't want us to replace the food. She was thankful we had saved all her other possessions.

Security

One beautiful Saturday morning in November I was sitting on my perch in the penthouse reading when a movement out of the window caught my eye. Civilians were wandering around in an inmate only area. I informed the room and several people hopped up on the bed to take a look. My friend April yelled out to them that the visitation area was on the other side of the building. The people yelled back their thanks but they had been there before and were just looking around.

This is a prison and they were just looking around. So much for security! We all had a great laugh that day watching them. No one official ever told them they were in the wrong place and I doubt anyone knew or cared.

The Boudicca of Lexington

If you are at all familiar with the Celtic warrior queen then you have a pretty good idea of what this girl looked like. Long flaming red hair and a temper to match! I didn't get to spend much time with her because she left about 2 months after I arrived. I adored her though. Everyone called her Red but her name was Roxy.

I've mentioned about bothering the chairs of those in top bunks. Roxy was the one who set the standard for this. Like many people, she used the chair to give herself a leg up to get onto her top bunk. If you messed with her chair she was either trapped in her bunk or you were between her and a nap. I watched a large number of people jump out of her chair and move away when they saw her coming. I didn't have to do that; I was allowed to use her chair.

Roxy is a cat person. She is such a cat person that her vet is on speed-dial. This came in handy one night when she was driving home and hit a cat. She called the vet and he suggested she try the nearest house. She did and they were not upset at all about the cat saying that "It wasn't the good one." She told me that was the closest she ever came to killing someone. The next day she sold her car because she couldn't face her cats after having hit one with the car.

Roxy was on Prozac and said it was to make her more social. She was pretty anti-social on the stuff so I can only imagine what she was like off it. She considered being in Atwood Hall as something of a vacation. She only had 8 months so I suppose that was as good a way to look at it as any.

Pay Your Parking Tickets

No matter how messed up your case might be or how bizarre you think your life has become, you will never come close to this level of bizarre in the real world.

There is a new arrival. I go down to collect her and give her the tour. The officer has been busy with a med transport so I start the tour and decide to do the paperwork when he is free. This new arrival doesn't look haunted; she looks amused. That's a new one for me but I begin the tour. I show her the cafeteria and then head down the staff hall. She stops me and asks to just go to her bunk. I explain that she will need to know where these places are the next day and she actually laughs. Then she explains that she is leaving in the morning. Now I'm the one confused. I do as she asks and take her to her bunk and then return to the office to get the paperwork and let the officer know that the tour was cancelled. He tells me her story.

Apparently she was on vacation in at Yellowstone National Park. She got a parking ticket and forgot to pay the $25. She had returned to her home in Florida. A few months go by and suddenly she is arrested by a Federal Marshall. She is then sent via plane at government expense to Wyoming to go to court over forgetting to pay the ticket. She pleads guilty and tries to pay the fine. Her payment is accepted but she is sentenced to 1 day in prison. She is then sent back to Florida. She ends up being designated to Atwood Hall. Once again the government pays to fly her, this time to Lexington. She spends the night and the next morning she leaves. The government pays to fly her back home.

The moral of this story is that the government will spend $50,000 to collect $25. This is why the nation is broke.

Escape!

Several of us actually escaped one afternoon. It was the fault of one of the dogs in the dog program. It had gotten loose and was heading to the highway. We chased after it and caught it before it could reach the road. When we were walking back we realized that we were way out of bounds and the others elected me to turn the lot of us in to the Officer. I went to the office, leaving the others in the lobby. I told him what happened and he wanted to know if we got the dog. I told him we had and he looked at us and pointed out that if we had escaped then we wouldn't be standing there and we should all go away rather than make him do paperwork about our delusional belief that we had escaped. We went away.

The Cell Phone was Ringing

One evening Valarie and I went down to get mail (I had a Jane package) and we had just cleared the stairway door when we heard the ringing of a cellphone. Cellphones, in case you were wondering, are strictly forbidden and an extremely serious violation of the rules. In fact it can add 2 years to your sentence and get you bounced to a medium security facility. Val and I went to her room because it wasn't our problem. The officer who heard it made everyone sit down, summoned another officer from the "A" building and everyone was patted down. They didn't find the phone that night but it put the officer is a foul mood for days. He questioned everyone about it when he saw them, including me. I was honest in telling him that I didn't know anything about it. I didn't. I had no desire to know about crap like that. It wasn't worth it to me.

A Sad Afternoon

You can get attached to people very quickly in a place like this. One such girl, Mel, was up on conspiracy charges. Her crime was that her little brother was selling pot and she didn't go to the police about it. Yes, that is a crime. He was sentenced to 20 years and she got 3. To make matters worse, because she was a "conspirator" they were not able to have any contact. No letters, phone calls or anything else. One afternoon I had just finished taking a new person on the tour and was returning to the office with the completed paperwork when I saw sirens and police cars zip past the outside headed to the "A" building. I walked into the office and Weiss told me to go to my room and stay there. He was hanging up the phone as he spoke. He asked if I had heard any of the call. I told him I hadn't and went to my room. When I got there, Mel was waiting for me. She gave me a hug and thanked me for being so nice to her. As she left, one of my roommates told me that Mel had taken a bunch of stuff and put it in my locker.

In prison you watch what gets put into your locker. I went to check and it was full of food. I mean a lot of food from the commissary. I didn't understand it until later that night.
Mel had been the one with the cellphone. Her little brother had one as well. He had been on the phone with her when his room was raided. His last words to her were "I'm busted." She knew it was only a matter of time before it was traced to her. Weiss unfortunately had to send her to county over it. Luckily she was not given additional time on her sentence but she never returned to Atwood Hall.

Escape! (Again?)

The best escape story I heard didn't happen at Atwood Hall. Atwood Hall has been known to have inmates sneak out, go to Wal-Mart and then come back. If you get caught you can expect an additional 10 years to be added to your sentence. No sale is worth it.

The escape story happened to the husband of the friend of a friend. He was in federal custody for being a master forger. He was apparently really good because he managed to forge his own release documents, send them to the prison and was released. It was nearly a year before anyone realized what had happened. By then he was in a non-extradition country.

Quotes on Prison Life

"I really hate weekends in prison....they are so boring." –Fran

"Stay away from that lesbian shit." –Tussey

"If you aren't a bigot when you get here you will be one before you leave." –Various

"They feed off of each other with each one making the problem worse and bringing out the worst in each of them." –Ms. Brown

"My meditation class lacks the proper ambiance for me to realize my meditating potential." –Popeck

"We were kicked out of crochet class for not appreciating the art of crochet. If we don't get it together we will be sacked from the knitting class for not appreciating the knits!" –G-Ma

"I've been a lesbian for more than 20 years. I came to this place and after just two days I've turned straight!" –April

"Piss me off and you will be a gruesome murder victim in my next novel." –Me

The definition of irony: The poem "The Road Not Taken" was taken from the poetry book in the library.

Inmate #1: I lost my ID
Inmate #2: Does it have your name on it?
Inmate #1: I think so…..

Who are your fellow campers?

When I left Atwood Hall this photo was given to me by the ladies pictured. They wanted it included in this book so that readers could see the typical camper at this prison camp.

Prison Cooking

The meals aren't bad here but sometimes you might prefer to just eat out of your locker. There is an amazing variety of things you can fix with ingredients you find in the commissary. Here are a few. None of these require food nicked from the kitchen though you might need to smuggle some milk to your room. If you can get some garden produce…well I won't tell if you don't!

Every floor has at least 1 microwave on it.

Pizza Rolls

These are hugely popular and very simple.
- 1 package of Tortillas
- 1 package of Summer Sausage
- 1 package of Pepperoni
- 1 package of Mozzarella Cheese
- 1 package of Cheddar Cheese
- 1 bottle of Spaghetti Sauce

Open and slice the meats and cheeses. Then spread some sauce on a tortilla, add meats and cheeses then roll up like a burrito. Microwave for about 2minutes or until the cheese melts.

For Hawaiian Wraps use ham, cheese and pineapple.

Pasta Salad

This is surprisingly good and was often made better with fresh veggies from the garden. I had a friend who worked in the garden and she was always smuggling stuff back for us.

- 3 California Vegetable Noodle Cups
- 1 package of Summer Sausage
- 5 packages of Ranch Dressing

Pour hot water into the noodle cups and allow them to cook for about 8 minutes. Drain off the water and dump the contents into a bowl. Dice the sausage and add it to the noodles. Add the ranch dressing and mix well. If you can, chill it.

Cinnamon Crunch Candy

This was so amazingly great that I still make it at home.

- 1 bag of Cinnamon Toast Crunch Cereal
- 10 pats of butter
- 5 bags of caramels (about 70 caramels)

Crush the cereal. Mix the butter and caramel together and melt in the microwave. Add cereal and mix. Let it set until cool and firm. We spread it in a lined box we had.

Dawn's Chocolate Cake

Dawn was the top go-to person for cakes. The Popeck had her make this one for my going home party.

- 1 package of Oreos
- 4 singles of Vanilla Pudding
- ¾ jar of Peanut Butter
- 2 bags of caramels (about 11 ounces)
- 10 Hershey's Kisses chopped
- ½ pint of Milk

Remove crème center from Oreos. Smash the cookies. Mix the milk, crème and pudding together. Stir in cookies. Press into bowl. Melt peanut butter and caramels together and then pour over the cake. Heat the cake for 1 minute in the microwave. Serve immediately and hide the scale.

Oreo Cookie Cake

A quicker and cheaper version of a cake is this one. It's still really good and it's fun to make one for the birthday of a friend.

- 1 package of Oreos
- 2 spoons of Peanut Butter
- Water or Coffee as necessary

Remove Oreo crème and set aside. Crush cookies and add enough liquid to make it doughy. Combine the peanut butter and crème then spread it on top of the cake.

Tuna Wraps

This is the second most popular wrap to make. There are several versions of this some plain and some fancy. This one version was my favorite.

- 1 Package of Tortillas
- 2 packages of Tuna
- Accent Sa-Son
- Mayonnaise

Mix everything together, spread on a tortilla and roll it up. No cooking necessary. Many people add chopped onions, relish, and even cheese.

Tips to Make Your Life Easier

There are several ways to make your life easier from the beginning. You can probably figure these things out quickly but it's easier if you go in with a plan. There are no real medical tests done for anything listed here. They tend to take you at your word.

Get a Soft Shoe Pass

I wore the steel toed boots exactly twice. I went to the commissary and bought tennis shoes the second day I was there. Ms. Sloan may have had her faults but she always allowed the orderlies to wear tennis shoes and skip the green shirt. I discovered that I had plantar fasciitis which is basically an inflammation in the tendon in your foot. You can either go in with this as an issue or mention it during your med evaluation. Mine hit before my official exam and that got me a soft shoe pass which means I never ever had to wear the boots. This condition is characterized by your foot (usually only one of them) being painful to walk on, like the muscle is too small for your foot) until you have walked on it for a bit in the morning. It's a pulling sensation in your foot and it never really heals. Until you go home. I haven't had a problem since I've been home. If you actually do have this problem you should get a pair of Reebok tennis shoes. The arch support in them helps to prevent this problem.

Have Asthma

Let them know during intake that you have asthma and you sleep with two pillows at home to help with your breathing. Tell them this and you get a second pillow. If you mention that you are worried about the stairs and your breathing you will also get an elevator pass.

It's Dark at Night

I told them this during the psychological intake. I also told them I couldn't stop crying. They gave me Prozac. Almost everyone is on some anti-depressant. I liked Prozac because you are allowed to self-medicate and I never actually had to take it. It also gave me a great excuse if anyone had said anything about my sleeping all the time (they didn't) or if some other issue had come up. I could have blamed the drug.

It's a Long Way Down

If you are afraid of heights you can get a bottom bunk pass. Actually many things will get you that including back issues. I was offered one because I really don't like heights but I was nestled against a wall and I liked being up in my perch.

Conclusion

You might have noticed a few themes here. Topping that list would be honesty and respect. If you treat others in this manner then your time in custody will be much smoother. The officers and staff members in Atwood Hall really do care and want to make your time there as easy as possible. Beyond that they just don't want to have to do mountains of paperwork. If you screw up, admit it then apologize. Most of the time it will be accepted and the matter will be dropped. You can't play these people. They have been working these jobs for decades and have handled far worse criminals than someone who is going to a federal camp. Be nice, do your time and move on with your life. Good luck to you and remember that this too shall pass.

My prayers are with you.

Further Reading and Websites

Prison Talk
This is without question the best website for inmates and their families.

Atwood Hall Website
This is the website for the Federal Medical Center in Lexington, Kentucky.

www.ingramcontent.com/pod-product-compliance
Lightning Source LLC
Chambersburg PA
CBHW060156290526
45789CB00003B/1062